COUNT IT ALL JOY

COUNT IT ALL JOY

How to Handle Problems and Trials

Barbara Lee Johnson

BAKER BOOK HOUSE
Grand Rapids, Michigan 49506

Fourth printing, November 1982

Revised edition issued 1980

ISBN: 0-8010-5104-5

Printed in the United States of America

While this book was written for the reader's help and blessing, it is also intended as the basis for group study in seminars, Bible studies or retreats. Cassette tapes of an actual Barbara Johnson teaching seminar covering the contents of this book are also available. If you are interested in Barbara's availability for your church or group, or if you desire a catalogue of her tapes, please write:

Barbara Lee Johnson
P.O. Box 6221
Orlando, Florida 32853

Contents

Preface

Accepting problems, difficulties, or heartbreak is not easy. It does no good to say there ought not to be sorrows or troubles. They do exist, and no amount of talking can erase or remove them from life. The basis of our worldly life is tragedy because sin has entered the human race. The Bible says, "Man is born unto trouble as the sparks fly upward" (Job 5:7).

In the last ten years literally thousands of Christian books have been printed in America. Why, then, do I feel the leading to add still another book? It is because I have become more and more aware that Christians, including myself, need to know how to handle the tragedies, crises, and hurts of life.

For fifteen years I have conducted a large weekly Bible class for women in Orlando, Florida. Week after week these women share their heartaches through prayer requests. It became obvious to me that most Christians have no greater capacity to endure trials than non-Christians. What was needed, I felt, was a practical handbook on how to deal with these rough spots in life. In fact, the more I prayed and studied the Word of God, the more convinced I became that God has told us everything we need to know about handling problems and going through trials. Our problem is that we do not know what God has to say,or we do not obey Him when He says it.

In preparation for this book, I searched through many Christian biographies and discovered that most of the great men and women of God underwent many trials and much suffering; yet they seemed to triumph over their difficulties with remarkable victory and unique joy. Most human beings do not share this unique joy. It was a joy that had nothing to do with outward circumstances, but was rather a constant and changeless emotion of the heart.

One such person was Madame Jeanne Marie Guyon, who lived in France at the beginning of the eighteenth century. She suffered immeasurable afflictions, yet became one of God's most glorious witnesses. While imprisoned by her own church leaders, she wrote that her time was passed in such great peace that she would be content to spend the rest of her life confined to her cell if that were the will of God. She also mentioned in her letters that she was enabled by the Lord to sing songs of great joy. In fact, her heart was so filled with this unique joy that her prison walls became like rubies to her eyes.

This woman experienced more joy in her life behind prison bars than most of us know during a lifetime of minor sufferings. Yet she was no supernatural saint, untouched by the trivialities of human life. She was but a simple, naive, unlearned French woman who had the rare ability to see God in her every trial and was enabled by His grace to live out her life in such rapturous adoration and love for Him that, to her, sufferings became necessary blessings.

The only qualifications I have for writing this book are a deep, abiding love for our heavenly Father and our Lord Jesus Christ, and a desire that His children may learn to count all their trials and problems a joy to the glory of God. Whatever is of help to you on these pages is there because the Holy Spirit has taken the words of His instrument and made them real to your understanding.

This book goes forth with my prayers that God might use some of these truths to help His children along life's journey.

BARBARA W. JOHNSON
ORLANDO, FLORIDA

There Is No Shangri-la

My brethren, count it all joy when ye fall into divers temptations; knowing this, that the testing of your faith worketh patience. But let patience have her perfect work, that ye may be perfect and complete, wanting nothing (James 1:2-4).

Rachel sat in my living room. Her face was ashen as she spoke in low, desperate tones. "My husband has left me. He's found another woman." She began to sob. "I can't go on."

"You must go on," I replied quietly. "You have three daughters to raise."

"But how will I face our children, our family, our church? How do you tell a board of deacons that their pastor has run off? How do you tell three young children that their father has deserted them? No, I just can't go on."

I tried to explain to her that the strength to face these trials lay not in herself but in Jesus Christ. She was so obsessed with her grief, however, that she would not listen.

One month later I heard the heart-breaking news that Rachel had taken an overdose of sleeping pills. She died in her sleep, alone.

The Existence of Suffering

Rachel is typical of many of us who are confronted with severe trials or difficulties. Some Christians refuse to even consider the thought that at some time in their lives they might be faced with broken health, separation from a mate, or any other type of unhappiness. They have convinced themselves that God intended their marriages to be perfect, their bodies healthy and fit, and their purses filled with wealth. Any other condition would be dishonoring to God. Thus, any trials that do occur not only upset them but also upset what they conceive to be God's perfect plan. A few Christians might even think that God has made a mistake in allowing such things to occur. The prevailing view today seems to be that heartache and suffering have no place in the Christian life.

As a result of such views, when our circumstances inevitably stray from perfection we feel that there is something wrong in our lives and that we must diligently search for whatever is causing such troubles. Once we find and remove the discordant element, our lives should become beautiful and trouble-free, as God so desires them to be.

Yet as human beings we cannot escape trial in our lives. The very process of being born makes us vulnerable to a certain amount of suffering. We all share disappointments, hurts, betrayals, and griefs from hundreds of different sources.

The Bible makes the principle of suffering clear in I Peter 4:12: "Beloved, think it not strange concerning the fiery trial which is to try you, as though some strange thing happened to you" (TLB). Even for Christians, there is no Shangri-la. There is no paradise on earth. A problem-free life simply does not exist.

Martin Luther, the son of a poor miner, was born into a life of abject poverty. He did not think it was unusual that God had allowed sufferings and trials in his life. He saw by the clear teaching of Scripture that it could not be otherwise.

The doctrine of suffering is at times ignored by Christians. To some, the suggestion of pain or suffering in conjunction with knowing Christ is unthinkable! It has been emphasized that Christ will provide us with health, wealth, and happiness in this world and in the next. As a result, we have not been emotionally equipped or spiritually prepared to deal with disaster or tragedy in human life.

But what does the Bible teach about this subject? It says, "Mankind heads for sin and misery as predictably as flames shoot upwards from a fire" (Job 5:7, TLB). "How frail is man, how few his days, how full of trouble" (Job 14:1, TCB) The Psalmist adds, "For my soul is full of troubles, and my life draweth nigh unto the grave" (Ps. 88:3, KJV). And Christ warned His disciples that "in the world ye shall have tribulation" (John 16:33, KJV).

The Bible contains the words *trouble* and *tribulation* over two hundred times! I mention this not to be morbid or to look at life from a "lower" point of view, but rather to face the reality of what God's Word actually teaches.

In a sense, we all live in two worlds—a real world which we must face every day, and a make-believe world of our imaginations, fantasies, and illusions. Many of us try to cope with our problems and overcome our difficulties through fantasy or make-believe. Some of us have lived so long in this fantasy world that we carry it over to our belief in God. Many people have come to consider God as a person who will not allow failures, disappointments, or heartbreaks.

Most of our early struggles as Christians involve our leaving this make-believe world, with all its illusions and fantasies, and beginning to cope with the real world. Unfortunately, when some people turn to Christ for salvation, they begin to build a new world of illusions. They believe that true Christians enjoy trouble-free lives and do not have to cope with the ordinary burdens that lesser Christians must endure. Their "Christian fantasy world" has no problems God will not solve, no sickness He will not heal, no circumstances He will not change.

To the wife whose husband has deserted her, they say, "He will come back."

To the father whose son is on drugs, they say, "He will be delivered."

To the mother whose child is ill, they say, "He will be cured."

But the husband does not return. The son is not delivered. The child dies.

What then? Must we assume that God's plan is not perfect after all?

God forbid!

The Lessons of Suffering

You see, even though the problem may persist, God is still in control. The words of Habakkuk, the prophet, may sound strange to us, yet what depth of understanding and love for God are expressed when he says:

> Although the fig tree shall not blossom, neither shall fruit be in the vines: the labor of the olive tree shall fail and the fields shall yield no meat, the flock shall be cut off from the fold, and there shall be no herd in the stalls: Yet I will rejoice in the Lord, I will joy in the God of my salvation (Hab. 3:17,18).

Habakkuk's faith and devotion were not based on what God would do or give, but rather on God Himself. In essence, Habakkuk was saying, "God, even if everything fails, if no problems are solved, if circumstances never change, I will still love You. I will still praise You. I will still count it joy just to know You."

This is not to say that God does not solve problems, heal the sick, or change circumstances. He can do all that and much more! What it does mean is that we cannot place God in a little box and say, "Now You shall act in this manner and in no other way."

Because suffering is such an integral part of human life, our Lord Jesus also suffered so that through suffering He also might learn obedience to the will of the Father. (See Heb. 5:8.) That is why it is safe to say to the suffering saint, "There is no pain with which our Savior cannot identify and thus give comfort in time of need."

Jesus knew He alone could comfort, for He said, "Come unto me all ye that labour and are heavy laden, and I will give you rest" (Matt. 11:28). He knew that the same Father who allowed His own Son to suffer would also prescribe suffering for us. He understands the ache of the human heart. He knows that sorrow, heartache, problems, and sufferings are the plight of all humanity; and in the heartache, in the sorrow, in the problem, He is the only one who can meet our need.

Our attempts to squirm out of our problems instead of accepting them as given by Him who loves us must indeed be grievous to God.

Christ promises to be with us throughout every pain and sorrow. Our attitude toward difficulties and sufferings may reveal the difference between *having* Christ and *professing* to have Him. It will certainly reveal the difference between that which is real and that which is unreal in our Christian lives. God wants us to know that if we have the Lord Jesus in reality, it will show not only in the way we live, but in our hearts as well.

When we belong to Christ, everything in our lives will be different. Our attitudes, our motives, and our actions will demonstrate that "If any man be in Christ, he is a new creation; old things are passed away; behold, all things are become new" (II Cor. 5:17).

The Fruit of Suffering

Sometimes we cannot see the reason behind our sufferings. God may not change our circumstances; He may change us instead.

Becky had been married seven years when her baby son drowned in the lake in front of their home.

"It's all my fault," she sobbed. "I left for just a moment to get some cookies in the house. The whole thing was my fault. God will never forgive me. I can never forgive myself."

Months passed. Nothing seemed to relieve Becky of her severe guilt. We told her of the power of Christ to wash away sin. We told her God had forgiven her, and now she must forgive herself. Nothing seemed to help.

One morning in Bible class, as we began reading a portion of God's Word, He tenderly opened Becky's spiritual eyes and heart to a new understanding of what had happened in her life.

As a mother with a heart bruised by grief, Becky read:

> What a wonderful God we have—he is the Father of our Lord Jesus Christ, the source of every mercy, and the one who so wonderfully comforts and strengthens us in our hardships and trials. And why does he do this? So that when others are troubled, needing our sympathy and encouragement, we can pass on to them this same help and comfort God has given us. You can be sure that the more we undergo sufferings for Christ, the more he will shower us with His comfort and encouragement (II Cor. 1:3-5, TLB).

"Could it be," she asked, "that God took my precious baby to heaven so that I might comfort other mothers who do not know Him with the same comfort He wants to give me?"

She answered her own question. "Yes! That must be why God allowed this to happen!"

I could sense that Becky at last had come to grips with this tragedy and with God. After class that day we sat quietly together with heads bowed before the God of all comfort as she willingly allowed Him to heal all the deep wounds of her grieving heart.

Then an amazing thing happened. Becky began to read the obituary column in the newspaper. Every time there was a notice that a baby had died, she would contact the grieving parents. Then she would tell them, "I would like to share with you the comfort I received from God when I lost my child."

We do not know how many souls she quietly led to faith in Jesus

Christ because of this great sorrow in her own life. Becky learned there is no Shangri-la; and by discovering God's hand in her trials, she was able to help others through the dark times of their lives.

But God had not yet finished with Becky. Through her acceptance of her suffering as the will of God, He had given her both a fresh understanding of Himself and a special ministry of her own. And much later—a precious new baby boy!

You see, God not only allows trials, but declares them to be instrumental in the development of character in human personality. "Now no chastening for the present seemeth to be joyous, but grievous: nevertheless afterward it yieldeth the peaceable fruit of righteousness unto them which are exercised thereby" (Heb. 12:11).

Could we say with the Psalmist, "I know, O Lord, that thy judgments are right, and that thou in faithfulness hast afflicted me" (Ps. 119:75)?

Let us pray for the ability to see with God's eyes. When we begin seeing things from His viewpoint, we have reached the first step in being able to count it all joy.

Prayer

O God, deliver me from the shallow waves into the depths of Your love. I am ashamed that I have constantly asked You to remove my problems when You have so lovingly allowed them in my life that I might have the ultimate joy of knowing You in all Your fulness. Try my faith, I beseech You, that I may hear Your voice, see Your face, and know and understand that You are God, and there is none else. For Christ's sake, Amen.

2

Why We Need Problems and Trials

For whom he did foreknow, He also did predestinate to be conformed to the image of his Son (Rom. 8:29a)

The Need for Reality

In spite of my extensive Christian background, I was totally unprepared for the first real trial I was forced to face. When the phone rang that Friday afternoon I expected it to be my husband. Instead, I heard the calm, unruffled voice of my doctor's nurse.

"Mrs. Johnson, your Pap smear came back positive. We have made arrangements at the Winter Park Hospital for you to have a biopsy tomorrow morning."

I managed to weakly reply, "Thank you. I will be there by seven o'clock." As soon as I hung up, I cried out to God, "Why me? I still want more children. I'm only thirty-one; I've just begun to live!"

After checking into the hospital the next morning, I told my story to my seventy-four-year-old roommate, Mrs. Anderson. She was dumbfounded.

"Well, I never!" she exclaimed. "How can a loving God do this to someone so young?" She turned her face to the wall and said she wanted nothing to do with a God like that.

Like many churchgoers, I had *professed* Christ but had never *possessed* Him in my life. It takes something drastic to make us realize we are living a fantasy. We wait until we get to our wit's end and there is nowhere else to turn. Then we cry to the Lord. Usually the trial comes from the outside, and we have no one on the inside to meet our need. That is when we realize we cannot handle the situation by ourselves.

That realization came to me as I dragged myself upstairs into the bedroom with my seldom opened Bible.

As I prayed, I knew I would have to cease every effort of trying to save myself and give up every claim of my life to Jesus Christ, leaving myself entirely in His hands.

"Lord, I've tried; but I can't make it without You. Now I'm asking You to come into my life. I'm asking You to save me. Help me, Lord; be merciful to me, a sinner!"

My sins swept over me like a tidal wave. I felt much as David must have felt when he cried out, "All thy waves and thy billows are gone over me" (Ps. 42:7). I was ready to give up when suddenly a remarkable thing happened.

"O God!" I gasped, "Speak to me! I've heard others say You spoke to them; so if You are real and if that is true, then speak to me!"

I waited for what seemed like hours, without hearing anything. All was still when I rose from my knees. As I did, however, I noticed the Bible had fallen open, and I began to read these words: "For I know the thoughts that I think toward you, saith the Lord, thoughts of peace and not of evil, to give you an expected end. Then shall ye call upon me, and ye shall go and pray unto me, and I will hearken unto you. And ye shall seek me, and find me, when ye shall search for me with all your heart" (Jer. 29:11-13).

I knew for the first time in my life that God had spoken to me personally! He had told me He had a plan for my life and that I would have the ultimate joy of finding Him in complete reality if I would search for Him with all my heart. My whole being responded, "Yes, Lord, yes, with all my heart!"

As I sit here in my bedroom many years after that glorious day, the Scripture verse from Jeremiah hangs on my wall. It was hand-lettered and given to me by a young couple who heard God speak and shared with me some of that wondrous love and joy that only He can give.

"This is for you, Barbara," they explained. "We have heard Him speak to us through your teaching of His blessed Word."

From the very beginning of my pilgrim journey, I learned the precious secret that God does actually speak through His Word to human hearts.

The Need for Understanding

Shortly after that miraculous day (when God transforms a soul, it is always a miracle), I was again quietly reading my Bible. I knew that surgery was ahead of me.

"You must be back in the hospital within three weeks," my doctor told me. "I'm allowing you to go home only because we need to build up your blood before operating."

My reading that morning was in the book of James. "My brethren, count it all joy when ye fall into divers temptations; knowing this, that the testing of your faith worketh patience" (James 1:2, 3).

This set me to thinking. Why should we count it joy when we must go through something difficult? Upon further research I discovered that, according to the Greek, the word *count* is a mathematical term. It means "to reckon upon, be absolutely convinced, count upon it." We might read the verse this way: "My brethren, be absolutely convinced, count upon it, reckon it to be all joy, when you fall into a trial."

I am convinced that if we would learn to do this, we would be able to say, "Thank You, Lord, for this heartache. Thank You for what You are allowing in my life."

When you are going through the trial, you seldom feel the joy; but if you will learn to reckon or count it all joy, the day will come when you will actually understand why God allowed it.

Recently, I had to go a step further. I found it incredibly difficult in the particular trial I was going through to count it *all* joy. Sometimes the heartache is a little more than you can take and you have to say, "Lord, I just can't count it all joy this time."

This brings us to the question of how to count a trial joy if we don't understand why God is allowing it. The scriptural answer is found in James 1:3, "Knowing this, that the trying (or testing) of your faith worketh patience." As I reread that verse, light began to dawn in my heart. My spiritual eyes were opened, and I saw that God was working something wonderful in me. That was why He was allowing this difficult time in my life.

What is patience? Why is it so valuable to God? Literally, it comes from a word meaning "suffering." Thus, we can understand that every believer is going to suffer at some time. This is because suffering is a basic ingredient of life. However, the difference for the Christian will be his attitude toward the trial because of his personal faith in Jesus Christ. From a biblical perspective, patience means "steadfastness of character, calmness under stress, or becoming Christ-like." Regardless of the burden of our trials, we are told by God to count it all joy.

I am often reminded of a woman who spoke to me after a meeting in Montgomery, Alabama. "I can count it all joy in every trial," she vowed, "except what people do to me. I don't mind what God allows; it's just what people do that I can't handle."

Strange, isn't it? Sometimes we fail to understand that God is the one who allows people to be people. He wants you to grow in faith. He wants you to be conformed into the image of Christ. He desires that your attitudes, your motives, and your reactions be Christlike through every trial. The only way this can be accomplished in our lives is through the testing of our faith by trials. Through them we can grow spiritually; and as we grow, our character will become steadfast, sure, and trustworthy for God. We will become people in whom God can see character, and who He knows will trust in Him no matter what happens.

It is well to know that God has only one desire for all His children. It is found in Romans 8:29: "For whom he did foreknow, he also did predestinate to be conformed to the image of his Son."

I am often asked, "What does God mean by predestination?" My answer has always been to simply drop off the "pre". God has a destination for you, if you belong to Him through faith in His Son.

What is our destination? The answer is obvious—to be conformed to the image of His Son, Jesus Christ; to be Christlike in every trial or testing. Every pain, every heartache, every problem, every disappointment is allowed by God to draw us closer to Himself and produce in us not only the right attitudes but the very likeness of Jesus Christ.

When I gave this definition to a group of women in Coral Springs, Florida, a woman exclaimed, "Barbara, I have been a Presbyterian for over forty-six years, and this is the first time I have ever understood predestination in a way I could apply it to my own life!"

The Need for Patience

I will always remember an afternoon I spent with Mrs. Lutie Cross, a dear saint of God who taught me much about the Word and how it relates to my own life. She was no pious, ethereal, holier-than-thou saint, but rather a down-to-earth, jovial woman who used to tell us "God calls us saints; He never said we were saintly!"

We who knew her were well aware that her sainthood was based solely on her relationship to Jesus Christ, who had invited her to be His very own.

"Mrs. Lutie, I want you to pray that God will give me more patience," I said.

Her deep brown eyes twinkled as she leaned over in her rocking chair and bowed her head.

"O, Lord," she prayed, "send this young woman trouble; send her trials; send her testing. Lord, bring her to the point where she can see no escape. Bring her to her wit's end."

Now this struck me as an inadequate and unacceptable prayer. Why, she had not even mentioned my need of patience to the Lord!

"Mrs. Lutie, I'm afraid you misunderstood me. I asked you to pray for patience, not for trials! I already have plenty of those!"

This dear old saint of God looked up into my face and said, "Barbara, learn this lesson well. The only way you can ever get patience is through suffering, trials, and testings. You see, the trying of your faith produces patience. There just isn't any other way to grow."

If I ever heard "holy laughter," it was when I shared some new heartache or trial with Mrs. Lutie. She would throw back her head with peals of laughter.

"Praise the Lord!" she would exclaim. "Isn't He wonderful? Think of what He is doing in your life! Mark my words, Barbara, God is going to use you, because He is refining you so severely!"

She was firmly convinced that all my troubles would make me grow. I was not quite so optimistic. If this was growing, it was the hard way of doing it. I was beginning to understand what was meant by the expression "growing pains."

Because God builds patience out of trials, you will discover that there will be times when you ask Him to give you patience in your trial, but it will get heavier instead of lighter. God wants results, and there is no easy road. As you grow and mature in Christ, you can look back and see that if God had not given you that trial, you would not have felt such a deep need to turn to Him.

The Bible teaches us that we will be able to hold our head high when we run into problems if we can just learn to endure and be patient. Listen to what God has to say in Romans:

> We can rejoice, too, when we run into problems and trials for we know that they are good for us—they help us learn to be patient. And patience develops strength of character in us

> and helps us trust God more each time we use it until finally our hope and faith are strong and steady. Then, when that happens, we are able to hold our heads high no matter what happens and know that all is well, for we know how dearly God loves us, and we feel this warm love everywhere within us because God has given us the Holy Spirit to fill our hearts with his love (Rom. 5:3-5, TLB).

In these verses, God is talking about our rejoicing in the fact that we belong to Jesus Christ. We rejoice not only because we are born again, but because we have trials, and these bring patience. Patience is character that God is building in you. It is an endurance quality. When you begin to get through your own hard times victoriously, then you will be able to help someone else. You can then say to others that no matter what problems they must endure, God can meet their need because He has met your own need. This is what the Bible calls experience.

Then something even greater will happen in your life. After the experience will come hope—the absolute certainty of mind and heart that God can meet every need in human life. Deep inside each person, no matter how prosperous or sophisticated he might appear, lies an emptiness that only Christ can fill.

You will know this from your own experience. That hope keeps you from being ashamed to make mention of His name. In fact, you may become so sure that God can meet other's needs that you will probably blurt it right out loud and give a personal testimony about the Lord Jesus.

Experiencing God's love in a testing time can give you a love for others which you have never felt before. Little wonder God sends trials. Little wonder James says, "Count it all joy." Think of all the glorious results!

Prayer

O, Lord, how perfect are Your ways. How little we understand them. Teach us Your way that we may grasp those things that are eternal. Open our eyes that we may learn to see that our problems and trials are good for us. Lord, help us to stop our murmuring and complaining. For Jesus' sake, Amen.

3

The Discipline of Seeing God in Difficulties

The eyes of the Lord run to and fro throughout the whole earth, to show himself strong in the behalf of them whose heart is perfect toward him (II Chron. 16:9).

Is God in Everything?

"God is not interested in my backyard fence." My host at the dinner table spoke in a matter-of-fact tone. "As I see it, this problem is between my neighbor and me. I can't see that God would be interested in anything like this."

Many questions came into my mind that evening. Was God interested in backyard fences? Are we who know Jesus Christ as Lord and Savior supposed to divide our lives into the secular and the sacred? Do we departmentalize our lives and say that Bible reading, prayer, and going to church are spiritual, but the ordinary activities of life—eating, sleeping, paying bills, buying groceries, and erecting backyard fences—have nothing to do with our relationship to God?

An earnest desire to find the answers to these questions led me to learn some vital lessons about seeing God in everything.

One of the hardest disciplines of the Christian life is seeing God's presence in every problem, heartache, sorrow, disappointment, or irritation. All too often we see the hand of God only in our joys and blessings, while failing to recognize Him in our difficulties.

The Bible clearly teaches that, for the children of God, everything that touches our lives is either directed or allowed by Him. It comes directly from His hands, regardless of the methods allowed by Him in bringing it about. It is a means by which God Himself can speak to us and teach us. Often, it is only through the pressures of circumstances that we hear God the clearest.

Our Lord Jesus had much to say about the least things of life. For example, He told His disciples, "Are not two sparrows sold for a farthing? And one of them shall not fall on the ground without your Father. But the very hairs of your head are all numbered. Fear ye not therefore, ye are of more value than many sparrows" (Matt. 10:29-31).

He also had a great deal to say about the ordinary events of life. Such mundane things as eating and drinking were discussed by our Lord. He said:

> Therefore I say unto you, take no thought for your life, what ye shall eat, or what ye shall drink, nor yet for your body, what ye shall put on. Is not the life more than meat, and the body more than raiment? Behold the fowls of the air; for they sow not, neither do they reap, nor gather into barns, yet your heavenly Father feedeth them. Are ye not much better than they? Which of you by taking thought can add one cubit unto his stature? And why take ye thought for raiment? Consider the lilies of the field, how they grow; they toil not, neither do they spin: And yet I say unto you, that even Solomon in all his glory was not arrayed like one of these. Wherefore, if God so clothe the grass of the field, which today is, and tomor-

row is cast into the oven, shall He not much more clothe you, O ye of little faith? (Matt. 6:25-30).

To a woman, "hairs on her head" and "raiment on her body" can be very important, especially when she has to be a platform speaker, constantly in public view. I still have many lessons to learn in this area of seeing God in everything, but I would like to share some of the discoveries I have made (and I would quickly add that I am still in the learning stage). The richness and fulness of these experiences are the attractions that keep leading me on towards the goal of seeing God in everything.

When I first began a ministry for Jesus Christ, it was in the form of a Bible class in my home. I remember well my first prayer to God about this class.

"O, Lord, if You will please send one person, I will teach Your Word." Only one came. I later learned to ask God for more—much more. We now have between three and four hundred women who meet each week to study His Word together.

At that time, my husband Don earned a very modest salary, but it was sufficient for the needs of two growing boys and a rather dilapidated two-story house we lovingly called home. (I used to call it my "what you ought to do house" because friends were always telling me what I ought to do to fix it up!)

As time went on, God began to enlarge my vision and my ministry. The need for nice looking clothes and a becoming hairdo became a real problem in my life. I knew God told me not to be anxious but with the number of speaking invitations increasing, I could not stretch our small income far enough to cover the things I needed.

My sewing room became the busiest and most frustrating room in the house. While I truly enjoyed being creative, I began to resent the time consumed at the sewing machine which could have been used for prayer and Bible study.

Demands in the ministry became heavier, and I began to pray

desperately for God to increase my husband's income. Instead, the dry cleaning plant he owned went into complete bankruptcy!

I had truly come to my wit's end. Then, early one Tuesday morning, I crept downstairs, knelt beside the living room sofa, and cried to the Lord.

"Lord, I don't know what to do or how to pray!" I whispered softly, "I can't see You in this dark time, but I need $15.00 for a permanent so my hair will look nice for the meeting on Thursday."

This was my first prayer to God for an ordinary, unspiritual thing. Later that same morning an unmarked envelope arrived in my mailbox; to my amazement, a $5.00 bill fell out of it!

When I visited my mother-in-law that same afternoon, she stopped me just as I was leaving. "Barbara, here is $10.00. I thought you might like to buy an Easter bonnet."

What an Easter bonnet! My heart went out to such a loving Father who had engineered circumstances so that I could discover for myself the reality of His being interested in every single thing—even the hairs of my head!

Several months later, two friends in the Bible class began to leave a $5.00 bill each week with the verse, "The very hairs of your head are numbered" written on the envelope. I knew they understood the same secret I shared with Jesus—my heavenly Father cares about the very least things in my life.

Not long after that transforming experience, another dear friend handed me a large sum of money and said, "Barbara, I would like to share some of your clothing expenses."

And the giving has grown and grown, just as the ministry has enlarged. God has met my every need. Surely King Solomon in all his glory could feel no better than I do when I stand before an audience to speak of the grace and wonder of simply knowing Jesus Christ and a heavenly Father who is in everything in my life!

Does God Really Care?

Our Father cares for us and about every least thing in our lives. He tells us not to be anxious about anything. He is our defense. He is on our side against the world, the flesh, and the devil. He also states that nothing can separate us from His love. His Word declares:

> . . . nothing can ever separate us from his love. Death can't and life can't. The angels won't, and all the powers of hell itself cannot keep God's love away. Our fears for today, our worries about tomorrow, or where we are—high above the sky, or in the deepest ocean—nothing will ever be able to separate us from the love of God demonstrated by our Lord Jesus Christ when he died for us (Rom. 8:38,39, TLB).

We also read: "The eyes of the Lord are in every place, beholding the evil and the good" (Prov. 15:3). "The ways of man are before the eyes of the Lord, and he pondereth all his goings" (Prov. 5:21), "The eyes of the Lord run to and fro throughout the whole earth, to show himself strong in the behalf of them whose heart is perfect toward him" (II Chron. 16:9).

If His eye is on the sparrow, and His eyes run to and fro throughout the whole earth, then surely we can trust Him with every difficulty in our own lives. Has He not promised to never leave us nor forsake us? Listen to the Psalmist as he speaks: "God is our refuge and strength, a very present help in trouble" (Ps. 46:1). Also, "I will say of the Lord, he is my refuge and my fortress, my God; in him will I trust" (Ps. 91:2).

We find the same assurance spoken by the apostle Paul in the New Testament: "If any man love God, the same is known of him" (I Cor. 8:3); and another statement: "The foundation of God standeth sure, having this seal: The Lord knoweth them that are his" (II Tim. 2:19).

Many other Scripture passages give us abundant proof that every detail of our lives is under the wise personal care of our heavenly Father. Nothing can touch us without His knowledge or consent. There are no "accidents" in a life deliberately placed in the hands of

God. When Paul wrote to the Christians of Rome, he stated, "And we know that all things work together for good to them that love God, to them who are the called according to his purpose" (Rom. 8:28).

This is a verse one great preacher called "a soft pillow for a tired heart." What a glorious thought! We can lie back on the pillow of the circumstances of our lives and know beyond a shadow of a doubt that even the wrong, the bad, and the unkind things are under the control of our Lord and can never touch us except with His permission and His knowledge.

The methods may originate with the enemy of our souls, and the means may be by people; but ultimately, by the time problems reach us, they are God's will for us in those particular situations. This is why Paul said, "In everything give thanks; for this is the will of God in Christ Jesus concerning you" (I Thess. 5:18).

No unseen power in heaven or earth, no person, no circumstance can touch us without our Father's permission. Someone once said that whatever comes to us must first be filtered through the fingers of God when we put our lives implicitly in His care.

We look at the life of Job as an example of this truth. When Satan appeared before the throne of God to dare him to test Job's remarkable faith, it was only through the permission of the sovereign God that Satan was allowed to touch him. (And God placed certain limits on that.)

We can see Job's faith grow by leaps and bounds as he trusted God and believed in Him through all the hard things allowed in his life. Ultimately, Job was victorious through faith!

The story of Joseph is perhaps the most outstanding of all Bible illustrations to reveal that God ultimately controls every event in our lives. Joseph was sold into slavery by his own brothers. These men were the means. The method originated from Satan, who is the father of all jealousy and lies. Yet Joseph later said to his brothers, "As for you, ye thought evil against me; but God meant it unto good" (Gen. 50:20a). God redeemed the evil done to Joseph and strengthened his faith, revealed divine wisdom, and saved a nation from starvation.

This doesn't mean we should accept evil conditions as inevitable and make no effort to resist or improve them. When a circumstance is clearly contrary to the will of God as revealed in the Scriptures, we are told to stand against the enemy and pray for God's intervention. God has brought about many wonderful changes in answer to this kind of prayer.

The important thing is that we not have a rebellious attitude toward the situation, as though God is being unfair to allow it to touch our lives. Many Christians feel like animals trapped in a cage of circumstance, constantly walking in a circle of self-pity. To them, God will remain silent.

How sad it will be to stand before the Lord one day and see what we might have become, what riches and glory we might have shared, what power and love we might have possessed; all opportunities that slipped away by our refusal to see God in our circumstances!

It will be cause for great lament to realize we dragged our feet through our problems when we might have flown over them on the wings of an eagle of trust. To be discouraged, downhearted, distressed, or disappointed when we might have had "joy unspeakable and full of glory" (I Peter 1:8)—what a tragic thought!

Will God Help His Sparrows?

I can still remember the afternoon I first met Jessie Mae. It was one of those hot, sticky days in late August. We were in the low-rent housing district, distributing food baskets with Gospel tracts tucked inside. My attention was drawn to a little fellow sitting on a doorstep eating popcorn.

"Do you like popcorn?" I asked.

"No ma'am," was the reply.

"You don't? I thought all little boys liked popcorn!"

"I hate it!" He jumped up and began to open a tattered screen door. "It's all I done ate for a long time!"

"How long?"

" 'Bout three days."

"Where is your mother?"

"She's inside—sick in bed."

I stepped inside the unkempt house. At first glance, Jessie Mae seemed too old to be the mother of the baby lying at the foot of the bed. I was shocked to learn that she was barely thirty-five years old.

"Do you have other children?" I asked.

"Yes ma'am—eight; but one has run off."

"Do you have a husband?"

"Yes ma'am—he's in jail. Had to call the sheriff. He gets drunk and beats me. Now ain't got money to buy the kids food." Then her tired eyes brightened. "But I knew the Lord would send someone to help. I done asked Him, and I knew He would."

Surely God's eyes were on His little fallen sparrow that day. Many Christians responded with "Let me help" when we took back the news. Others said, "We will pray," and they did. As the weeks and months passed, the story was repeated over and over again. Husband Willie would work for awhile, then come home drunk, and the beating would start again. Time and time again Jessie Mae would call for help.

"Jessie Mae, how can you go on?" I asked one day in exasperation.

" Cause one day God is gonna save that man, and I ain't gonna give up!" she replied.

Two years later, I sat in the small, neat living room of Jessie Mae's new home. Outside, her redeemed husband Willie was busy planting his garden, humming as he hoed the ground.

The baby, now an active three-year-old, was napping in the small bedroom off the kitchen. We were reading together the eleventh chapter of the Gospel of Matthew, when we came to this verse: "The blind receive their sight, and the lame walk, the lepers are cleansed, and the deaf hear, the dead are raised up, and the poor have the gospel preached to them. And blessed is he, whosoever shall not be offended in me" (Matt. 11:5, 6).

I paused for a moment. Jessie Mae's eyes filled with tears as she glanced around the bright, cheerful room, then outside toward Willie.

"That's the way it always was with Jesus and me," she said softly. "All them years I wasn't never offended by one thing He done."

I knew Jessie Mae had learned the secret of seeing God in everything, and I have never forgotten the glory of that moment.

Prayer

Precious Father, forgive us for being blind to Your Presence. Open our eyes that we may behold You in every circumstance of our lives. Let us heed Your voice in every situation. May we never be offended in You. Amen.

4

The Value of Praising God in Problems

Giving thanks always for all things unto God and the Father in the Name of our Lord Jesus Christ (Eph. 5:20).

It was early spring in the mountainous regions of Pakistan. A young missionary mother sat heartbroken at her breakfast table as the first rays of sunlight began to appear across the horizon. With a grieving heart she had just loaded her four children into a rickety old school bus to make the perilous journey over narrow roads and high mountain passes to attend school at the missionary compound hundreds of miles away.

The youngest child could not understand why Mommy and Daddy must send her away. After many hugs, kisses, and tears, the young mother watched her husband drive the old bus down the narrow road.

Returning to the house, she began her lonely vigil. It would be well over two weeks before her husband would return and she would know that their precious children were well and happy. As her tears began to flow, the God of all comfort manifested Himself.

"I looked up," she wrote, "and among the mail we had received the night before was a copy of the March issue of *The Alliance Witness.* Numbly, I began to leaf through the magazine when my eyes fell on your article, "The Value of Praise." As I read, I began to do as you suggested and "praise the Lord." A comfort and joy such as I never dreamed possible began to lift my heart and fill my being. I am writing you this letter to thank you for sharing this message from God to His children all over the world."

Learning to Praise

It is of the utmost importance that we learn the value of praising God through our trials if we are to experience the comfort and joy of the Lord in our hearts.

One day I began to obey Ephesians 5:20, "Giving thanks for all things unto God and the Father in the name of our Lord Jesus Christ."

I soon discovered "all things" to be a pretty large dose to swallow. It was then that I decided that rather than try for a day at a time, I would try for a moment at a time, then minutes, then hours. To my delight, I found that praising God becomes a habit—and what a glorious habit! My whole life took on a glow, and what used to bring discouragement now brings only joy.

There is no way to measure the true value of praise. It alone is the proof that we are really satisfied in the heart. When people see us delight in and praise the object of our pursuit, they know that (at least to us) it is a treasure; and often, they are attracted to seek the same for themselves. Manufacturers and merchants use this truth almost exclusively in attracting buyers for their wares. A satisfied customer who praises their product will do more to promote sales than anything else.

With this thought in mind, we can easily see what a heart full of praise to God could do to attract others to the Lord Jesus Christ, and to the love of God which is found in Christ alone. Nothing will draw men and women to Christ more quickly or effectively than one whose heart is filled with enthusiastic praise.

The habit of praise in the Christian's life, when compared to the average person's life, is like a glorious spring morning compared to a dull, drab, winter day. Praise changes a cold, bitter heart into one filled with exquisite happiness and joy.

We often miss this quiet and pure way of worshiping God in favor of the more exciting, emotional activities so prevalent in present-day Christianity. Yet the Scriptures reveal that praise in every circumstance of daily life is one of the simplest and most direct ways of worshiping and glorifying God which is available to the believer. I am constantly amazed at how quickly first inclinations toward discouragement vanish when I lift my heart to Jesus and praise Him for the wonderful privilege of just knowing Him and loving Him.

Praise can and should be in the heart and on the lips of every soul who has heard Christ say "Thy sins be forgiven thee." His Word commands us to praise Him. "By him therefore let us offer the sacrifice of praise to God continually, that is, the fruit of our lips giving thanks to his name" (Heb. 13:15). Every single thing in our lives should draw from our lips praises to our heavenly Father. Is it not enough to know that His way is perfect? For this alone we should praise Him continually. Praise should pour from our lips as the mighty rivers rush into the sea. Praise to God should be our meat and drink, our breath, our very life.

God dwells in the praises of His people (Ps. 22:3). We are overcome with awe when the realization of this truth first reaches the depths of our hearts. How great You are, our God, that You who are the Creator, the high and lofty One who inhabits eternity, whose name is holy, delights in the praises of Your people! Oh, the glory of praising our redeemer! Oh, the delight of singing His praises until the heart is enraptured with His love!

True praise seeks only to glorify God—never to draw attention to one's self. True praise is a natural outflow, pouring from the lips over the quiet, commonplace things of life. Because praise glorifies God, He will reveal Himself as our ever-abiding refuge when our lips praise His name continually.

How many Christians live in unhappiness even though they are convinced that they shouldn't live this way. The revelation of divine truth declares the believer to be partaker of the divine nature (II Peter 1:4), a partaker of Christ (Heb. 3:14), and of the heavenly calling (Heb. 3:1). Those who have received Christ have been given the authority to become the sons and daughters of God Himself (John 1:12). Surely a Christian has every reason to praise God.

In light of these glorious truths, it is sad indeed that many believers rise to a certain level in Christian experience and then gradually slip back to lower levels. Could it be that the one thing lacking is this habit of praising God for everything in life? Is it not probable that because we do not praise Him for the "now," we are unable to trust Him for the "tomorrows"?

Life is made up of a multitude of small things. It is here that I am learning the art of praising God in everything. If I praise Him this moment, will He not keep me the next and the next? It is the attitude toward the little things of the moment, not the vast issues of the age, that weaves the fabric of a man's life. A man who faithfully praises God for the little things will find that God gives him the great things.

The apostles John and Paul, Brainerd and Simpson, praised God in the least things, and because of this, God granted to them the great things.

Does your heart seem cold and distant toward your loving Father? Do disappointment and discouragement seem all too often your portion? Is the sweet presence of Christ no longer real to you? Then listen to the words of the Psalmist as he woos us into the presence of the King: "Come before his presence with singing. Enter into his gates with thanksgiving, and into his courts with praise; be thankful unto him and bless his name" (Ps. 100:2, 4). Could anything be more simple and clear? Enter into the joy of your Lord today. Claim this moment the sufficiency of Christ to satisfy every need of the soul. Cultivate praise. Never cease to give Him praise. Praise Him moment by moment, until life becomes a symphony of praise.

If there are times, and there will be, when the feelings are dull and the experience of His presence is not as much as you could wish, continue to praise God for the life of untold blessedness to which you have been called. Avail yourself of every opportunity of exercising praise. Even when you are overtaken by sin and your heart is disturbed, look into the face of your loving Savior, confess your sin, and praise Him for His forgiveness.

We can all begin this moment, to praise our Father until the abundance of joy overflows upon our lips and we will continually offer the sacrifice of praise to our God. "Let everything that hath breath praise the Lord" (Ps. 150:6).

The Results of Praise

I could not close this chapter without telling you about what happened in Elaine's life. On the surface, all seemed fine. Actually, she was far from happy. Her husband George had an excellent government job. They had two wonderful children. When I first arrived at the lovely colonial brick home surrounded by several acres of wooded landscape, I was amazed at the opulence. As I took the "Cook's tour" through her home, Elaine expressed pride and joy over such spacious surroundings.

"Barbara, do you remember when we lived in Orlando? Our home in that subdivision was so tiny. I am grateful to God for this home and my two children; but frankly, that's as far as it goes!"

"What do you mean, that's as far as it goes? Have you forgotten that you and George belong to Christ? Have you forgotten that God has saved your two precious children? Doesn't that count for anything?"

"Yes, I am very grateful to God for that; but Barbara, my life has become a hell on earth! George never speaks to me. For weeks, even months, he hardly says a word. I've read many Christian books on marriage, and tried to do everything they suggest, all to no avail! I have begged him to go with me to our minister or a marriage counselor, but he refuses. We never have any friends here because he doesn't want them. He forbids the children to have their friends over, so I am constantly driving them to other homes to play. At dinner, he never says a word. If I ask him how he enjoyed his meal, he will tell me, 'If I don't like what you prepare, I will let you know.' I am absolutely desperate! I feel like someone in a cave who can't escape! What am I going to do?"

I knew, of course, that George needed professional help. A Christian psychologist could diagnose his problem, but that would not help Elaine in her present distress.

"Let's pray about it right now and ask God to establish our thoughts so we will know what you are to do," I said.

Since I had to speak at a Christian Women's Club meeting later that evening, we prayed a quick petition to our heavenly Father for some portion from His Word which would help Elaine.

Later that night, I lay in bed in the beautiful surroundings of Elaine's guest bedroom. I was exhausted from the long flight and the large meeting.

"I'll just wait until morning to talk to God about Elaine," I thought.

But the Lord had other ideas! After several hours of tossing and turning, I sat up and turned on the light.

"O.K., Lord, I know You want my attention; so here I am!" I sighed.

The thought came to me to read in Psalms. But where in Psalms? I knew one of the main themes of the psalms was praise. I also knew they were filled with David's cries for deliverance from all his troubles.

"Now, Lord, You know I can't read all these psalms tonight. Besides, I have to be up early to speak at a ten o'clock meeting, and again at noon. You know I need some rest."

So into the psalms I went. I read Psalm 1, then Psalm 2. Still no thoughts established.

"Oh, well, here goes! I'll read Psalm 3. Wait a minute! Didn't Elaine say she felt like she was in a cave with no escape? Wasn't David in a cave once when he fled from King Saul? Didn't he write about it?"

Eagerly I turned to Psalm 57, since I had delivered a message on it only a few weeks before. I quickly read to verse 7, and there it was—my answer for Elaine! "My heart is fixed, O God, my heart is fixed: I will sing and give praise"; and again in verse 9: "I will praise Thee, O Lord, among the peoples; I will sing unto Thee among the nations."

The next morning, after George and the children had left for the day, I told Elaine I felt God had given me a verse for her. We read the psalm together.

"But, Barbara, I can't sing and give praise. I just can't!"

"That is just the point, Elaine. You must fix your heart to will to do it. Don't you realize that whatever we will to do is what we do? You must will to praise God even though you don't feel like it. Let's ask the Lord to help you to at least try to praise Him, and see what happens. Will you agree?" We held hands and prayed.

Several months later I received a letter from Elaine.

"I would like to tell you the problem has cleared up," she wrote, "but that would not be the truth. George is still the same, but something very strange and exciting has happened to me! I began to force myself to say the words 'Praise the Lord' and 'Thank You, Lord.' I'll admit, I did not feel like saying it, and, at times, even felt resentful toward God that He would want me to praise Him when He did not seem the least bit concerned with my problem. Then I began to write down a list of things for which I could praise the Lord. After several days, I found I was thinking of things right off the top of my head to thank Him for. By the end of the second week, I began to want to praise the Lord. By the close of the third week, I was delighted to praise the Lord for everything! Now, all the depression has lifted, and I am truly out of my cave! Praise the Lord!"

Won't you will to praise the Lord in your problems? Think of the difference it will make in your life!

Prayer

Lord, teach me to praise You. Forgive me for missing this quiet and glorious way of worshiping You. Give me a heart that is grateful to You for my very breath. Lord, teach me to praise Your blessed Holy name! Amen.

5

The Acceptance of Faith

Dear brothers, is your life full of difficulties and temptations? Then be happy, for when the way is rough, your patience has a chance to grow. So let it grow, and don't try to squirm out of your problems. For when your patience is finally in full bloom, then you will be ready for anything, strong in character, full and complete (James 1:2-4, TLB).

Dick and Beth spent many long hours in prayer. They had taken their youngest son Joey from one doctor to another, only to be told the same tragic news. Joey was retarded. There was nothing that could be done.

"We prayed for Joey for seven years," Dick reflected, "and during all those years we felt that if we could only pray the prayer of faith, healing would be granted. Then one day our two older children began to beg us for something that we could not possibly give them. As their father I earnestly wanted to give them what was best, but this was something beyond my control. It grieved me to have to say 'no' to them. It was then that God seemed to show me that it was wrong to keep on pressing Him for something if it was not in His plan to grant it. Beth and I were actually praying, 'Thy will be changed' instead of, 'Thy will be done.' That day we learned to accept Joey just as he was. Our grief began to turn into joy as we learned that it was only in acceptance that we found peace."

As I listened to Dick's testimony, I knew he had discovered an answer to one of the most perplexing questions in a Christian's mind and heart.

The Experience of Faith

Perhaps you have wondered why, with the whole Bible in your hand and Jesus Christ in your heart, your life is faint and feeble when trials come, and lacks the fulness of love and joy you had expected. Why is it that your own life seems void of that unique joy you sometimes see in other Christians?

Most of us would agree that *"the joy of the Lord is our strength"* (Neh. 8:10), but how to have that word *joy* be more than a verbal expression seems to be a mystery. We know water can't rise above its own level. We can work ourselves up into a frenzy, but why bother? We either have joy or we don't, and all the talking will not change the inward attitude of the heart. The fruit is determined by the tree, and the true worth of the tree is determined by the fruit it bears. We know we ought to count trials a joy, but how to do it is another matter.

In order for you to get the most out of this book, there is one fundamental requirement. Begin right now to put into practice what you are learning. The only way to learn is by doing. Faith is active, never passive. If you desire to count it all joy when you go through a trial, then you must act on what you are learning. Experience is knowledge that sticks in your mind.

It will probably be hard to apply what you are learning to every little difficulty. Yet the actual experience of going through it produces the joy. In other words, no experience, no joy! It is easier to read a book about what we ought to do than to actually do it! God wants you to have joy that nothing can destroy. He wants you to learn how to transform your sufferings into real spiritual blessings.

The first way to turn trials into blessings is through the acceptance of faith. But God is talking about actual faith, not merely acceptance. Anyone can learn to accept a situation when he goes through a trial, but God is speaking in the Book of James about the acceptance of faith, and there is a difference. To accept a circumstance, as Joseph did, even though it seemed all wrong, and still be able to see God in that circumstance, is the acceptance of faith which the Bible talks about.

As a new Christian, I had the usual ups and downs. During one of my down periods, I was asked by someone how I could prove my faith. I gave my usual reply "God said it; I believe it; that settles it!" My inquirer was satisfied with my answer, but I found it did not satisfy me. How could I really prove my faith? If you were asked to prove your faith, how would you go about it?

The first proof of faith is the acceptance of every trial and testing. The basis of faith is the Word of God, but proofs of faith come from living the life. It is in love that our Father sends the trials, making the world around us dark and unattractive, so that we might see the glory of God in the face of Jesus Christ. The unchangeable objective of our heavenly Father's actions is that we might prove for ourselves His faithfulness and the reality of our own faith in Him.

God tells us in the Word that all spiritual living is based on faith. Everything else may fail, but if your faith in Him stands, your whole spiritual life will stand. All else will fail if your faith fails. Satan's fiendish desire is to destroy your faith in Jesus Christ. Since the Garden of Eden, he has been trying to create in the mind of man the devastating thought that God does not really love man. His plot is to make it appear as though God does not hear or answer prayer.

I have a friend whose home burned to the ground last year. She told me that the only things which survived the fire were her diamonds, precious jewels, silver, and gold. Everything else was destroyed. When we go through the fires of trials and testings, that which is left is our basic faith—the precious substance of which our relationship to Jesus Christ is made. The songwriter said it well: "The flames shall not hurt thee; I only design thy dross to consume, thy gold to refine."* The apostle Peter tells us how we might graduate with honors from the school of faith: "That the trial of your faith being more precious than gold that perisheth, though it be tried with fire, might be found unto praise and honor and glory at the appearing of Jesus Christ" (I Peter 1:7).

Do not be content to live in the shallow stages of the Christian life! Tune your spiritual faculties toward experiencing the living presence of God. Know and count upon this fact, that trials are necessary for growth in Him. He is ever living, speaking, loving, and ready to make Himself known unto you.

I admit that there are many things that are unexplainable. In Psalm 139:12, God says that the darkness and the light are both alike to Him. He is still God even in the dark, confusing things of life. Even if we don't understand, will not the end explain? Can we not accept what He has allowed? We must learn to trust in Him when we do not have an answer, when we do not understand. Learn that even in the darkest night the aching heart can find its solace in God.

The Testing of Faith

Have you ever had one word in the Bible jump off the page at you as the answer to a problem you had been struggling with? I would like to share with you my discovery of the little word *when*. As a young Christian, I would go through one trial and gain a little ground, then another would hit me. Sometimes I would barely be back on my feet from the previous trial when a new one would come along. It seemed every rug I stood on was pulled out from under me, and I would inevitably fall. I would earnestly pray,

*From "How Firm a Foundation," "K" in John Rippon's *Selection of Hymns*, 1787.

searching my heart for some unconfessed sin. I decided I must be the worst, most sinful Christian who ever named the name of Christ. Worst of all, I did not seem to be learning anything through the trials. It was just a matter of holding on until it was over.

First there was sickness, then terrible financial struggles, then the agony of being misunderstood by other believers (which is by far the most difficult affliction). Each one came as an unexpected fiery dart because I had not seen that little word *when*. You see, I didn't know that God's Word teaches us to expect trials and testings. I thought the devil had gotten the upper hand and was sneaking these trials in on me without God's knowledge or permission. So I thought I had to go to God each time and tell Him I was having a trial, so He would be sure to help me get out of it. One morning, I was reading these words in James: "Count it all joy, my brethren *when* you meet various trials" (James 1:2, RSV). As I read, I saw the word *when* with the eyes of faith, and my heart fairly leaped for joy! God was saying to me, "My child, your faith will be tested. It shall be tested again and again. Count on it; for if faith is to grow, it must be tested. But I want you to know that there will be a crown of life waiting for you when you go through the trials and glorify Me in them."

Again, that same morning I read in Isaiah: "*when* thou passest through the waters, I will be with thee; and through the rivers, they shall not overflow thee: *when* thou walkest through the fire, thou shalt not be burned; neither shall the flame kindle upon thee. For I am the Lord thy God, the Holy One of Israel, thy Savior" (Isa. 43:2,3).

God does not say *if* you go through the waters or fire; rather, He says *when* you go through them!

Most of us want conditions changed because we don't like what God has ordained for us. I remember talking to a woman in Atlanta, Georgia, who said, "You mean God may never change my husband? I may have to live with him in this situation for the rest of my life?"

"I can say this much," I replied, "until you can accept him just like he is, God probably won't change him."

Many say to me, "But you don't understand what I am going through. No one understands." This is talking against the will of God! We want everything changed. We simply won't face the fact that we have this attitude of rebellion against the will of God!

Through these testings we grow in patience and acceptance until we no longer rebel against the will of God.

At a recent *Count It All Joy* retreat, I invited every woman there to commit her whole life to Christ, desiring God's perfect will. I spoke to those attending, "God allows you to have that husband. He allows you to have that situation in your home. God allows you to have those particular children because He wants you to have the acceptance of faith, not rebelling against His will for your life."

On the Sunday morning following our Saturday night campfire of commitment, I heard a tap on my door. It was a woman who had poured out her heart to God the night before. With tears in her eyes she told me what He had taught her during the early morning hours.

"I had to accept the fact that God's way is always perfect, and He never makes a mistake," she sobbed. "My home situation has been like a yoke around my neck because I did not like what God had allowed in my life and would not accept it. Then this morning I told the Lord I would accept whatever His will was for my life. I feel a liberty and freedom in this acceptance like I have never had before. I am willing to do anything that is God's will for me from this moment on."

Many of us have chronic problems. Some may be physical limitations that are quite bothersome. But like the apostle Paul, God wants to bring us to the point of crying, "Lord, when I'm weak, that's when I'm strong!" God told Paul, "I am not going to relieve you of this burden; I will allow you to carry it, so you can discover for yourself that My grace is sufficient to meet your every need." Paul responded that he would glory in the weakness—even praise God for it! In accepting it, he would no longer rebel against the will of God in his own particular trial. In the same way, God allows us to go through trials so we will discover for ourselves the joy of acceptance of faith.

Often, when the trial or problem originates from others, we refuse to count it all joy and seek to "get back" through revenge. I have been through many kinds of trials, but for me, nothing compares to the suffering felt when other believers hurt, misunderstand, or mistreat me. We can say, "Thank You, Lord, because I know you allowed this in my life. I know this illness is from you." But when someone hurts us, we find it harder to accept it as coming from the Lord. Yet God says to count anything and everything that comes into your life, no matter how hard it is, all joy!

To count every trial as joy requires a deep desire in our hearts for this acceptance of faith. Desire is the motivating energy of the heart. Without desire there can be no reality, for it is the very touchstone of faith. Without desire to believe, there can be no belief. Without desire to pray, there can be no prayer. Without desire to accept something from God, there will be no acceptance.

But nothing slips away more easily than desire. Do you remember your delight in Christ's love and salvation when He first called you to Himself? Do you recall how your heart overflowed with joy as you earnestly and deeply desired to follow Him? But have you now succumbed to the monotonous duties of everyday life, with all of its problems and burdens? Instead of your desire deepening, has it become faint and almost disappeared?

How little we have understood our great need of reality in Christ! How little we have realized that acceptance of faith is the only path to full communion with our beloved Lord! We must desperately want to learn to accept all from Him! Singleness of purpose must possess us! "This one thing I do," said the dauntless spirit of the apostle Paul. But I think Solomon said it best of all: "let thine eyes look right on, and let thine eyelids look straight before thee. Ponder the path of thy feet, and let all thy ways be established. Turn not to the right hand nor to the left . . ." (Prov. 4:25-27).

This is singleness of desire. If the joy and lasting fruit of this blessed life is to be ours, we must learn this deep desire for the acceptance of faith.

Prayer

Oh, my Savior, I must know You in all Your fullness! I must be wholly Yours! Give me this deep desire for the acceptance of every single thing from Your blessed hands. Teach me that only in acceptance will come peace. Amen.

The Prayer of Faith

If you want to know what God wants you to do, ask him, and he will gladly tell you, for he is always ready to give a bountiful supply of wisdom to all who ask him; he will not resent it. But when you ask him, be sure that you really expect him to tell you, for a doubtful mind will be as unsettled as a wave of the sea that is driven and tossed by the wind; and every decision you then make will be uncertain, as you turn first this way, and then that. If you don't ask with faith, don't expect the Lord to give you any solid answer (James 1:5-8, TLB).

One day my neighbor and I were having our morning Bible study.

We were bowing our heads to pray when suddenly Ann looked up and said, "You know, Barbara, my pastor said something last Sunday that really impressed me. He says faith is *now!* Right now!"

In the days that followed, I could not get this thought out of my mind. Yes, I thought, faith *is* right now! Faith always deals with the present moment. This is, perhaps, one of the hardest concepts for the Christian to grasp. We fret about our yesterdays and worry about our tomorrows, but very few Christians experience the moment-by-moment reality of a "now" faith. Few have incorporated this fundamental concept of faith in their lives: "I believe in God right now; I trust in Christ this moment."

I had just taught a Sunday school class on this subject of a "now faith" when a leading layman in the church said to me, "Barbara, I have somehow always thought of God as doing something for me tomorrow or next week or next year. After all these years as a Christian, it has suddenly dawned on me that faith is in the present moment!"

In our lesson that morning, we had discussed an incident in the life of our Lord concerning His healing the man who was born blind. The religious people wanted to keep him out of the synagogue because he wouldn't keep quiet about his healing, but Jesus sought him out and asked, ". . .Dost thou believe on the Son of God? He answered, and said, Who is he, Lord, that I might believe on him? And Jesus said unto him, Thou hast both seen him, and it is he that talketh with thee. And he said, Lord, I believe. And he worshiped him" (John 9:35-38).

The blind man did not wait until next week or next month to believe in the One quietly speaking to him. He reached out in faith at that very moment, and believed.

It is not the same way with us. We often seek Him at our meetings, and we search for Him in the books we read, thinking that somehow, some way, we will discover the reality of His Presence. All the while our Lord is speaking, if only we would listen: "My child, I am here with you this moment, this very moment. Recognize My presence, and believe in Me right now."

In prayer, more than in any other area in the spiritual life, we must learn the reality of believing in the present moment. There is no way to please God without a present tense faith. The human mind seems unable or unwilling to grasp this simple fact. Yet all the attitudes of the Christian life must develop from this principle until it becomes a reality. Deeper knowledge of God comes from passing through the lonely valleys of trial and suffering, for there we can discover the eternal secret that *God is.*

The Bible says faith is not only past (Christ died for my sins), and future (He shall deliver me from the wrath to come), but, above all, present (He is here right at this present moment, in the middle of this problem).

All day long you are making choices about whether to believe in Jesus in some particular thing and whether to count on God's presence at that very moment. The writer to the Hebrews put it this way: "Without faith it is impossible to please God; for he that cometh to God must believe that he is, and that he is a rewarder of them that diligently seek him" (Heb. 11:6). Deliberately encourage your mind to dwell on this glorious truth: God is, and He is a rewarder. True faith is always active—never passive!

There is not a situation in human life which He cannot take care of if you will believe Him this moment. He will meet you in every problem if you will put your trust in Him. God will allow your faith to be tried so that all of the stiff and lazy "put-off-until-tomorrow" qualities about your faith will begin to fade away, and in their place will come a holy desire to grow deeper and deeper in His love this present moment.

Faith Is Answered Prayer

I might never have learned the lesson of the prayer of faith if it had not been for Margaret Arndt, her sister Katie, a canary, and Belk's Department Store. It all began on the glorious day that Margaret turned her life over to Jesus Christ. One of her deepest desires was that her sister Katie would come to know and love the Savior as she did. The day finally came when sister Katie, fresh from her German homeland, arrived in the States. She was not particularly interested in the Bible class, yet Margaret brought her, week after week, to hear the claims of Christ on her life.

One day, Katie went to Belk's and bought a beautiful yellow canary. The saleslady just happened to be from Katie's hometown in Germany. (We who belong to God know that "just happened" actually means "just ordained" by Him!) As the weeks rolled by, Katie's love for the canary grew, and her interest in the things of the Lord diminished.

After several months, a terrible thing happened. Katie's canary flew away!

"Margaret!" she cried, "My beautiful canary is gone!"

"If you only knew my blessed Lord, you could ask Him to bring the canary back!" responded Margaret.

"If your God will bring back my canary, then I will believe in His Son," Katie vowed.

A few moments later, my telephone was ringing.

"Barbara, we must pray and ask God to return Katie's canary!" exclaimed an excited Margaret.

She then told me the story of how Katie's bird had flown away and what Katie had vowed before God. At that moment, my faith was down to nothing.

"Now, Mrs. Arndt," I explained, "God did not say He would bring back canaries. Why, that would be next to impossible! He just didn't promise to do a thing like that!"

"I can see you do not believe!" she responded icily. Then, in half English and half German, she admonished me for not trusting in a God who could do anything, especially for the soul of her sister Katie.

Nearly two weeks later I learned my lesson on the prayer of faith. Margaret had prayed constantly that God would bring back the canary so that her beloved Katie would believe in Him. My deep concern was that if the bird did not return, it would not only turn Katie farther away from God, but Margaret's faith (which was so new) would begin to falter. I should have known better! This lovely German woman who had found Christ late in life believed every word God said in His Word.

"Didn't He say if you would ask anything *believing*, He would do it?" she asked.

It was a tremendously excited Margaret who phoned me that day.

"Barbara! God brought back Katie's bird!"

"How?" I exclaimed.

"The bird flew to Belk's, and the German saleslady remembered Katie, phoned her, and told her the canary was back at the store! Praise God, Barbara! Now Katie will believe in Jesus! I just know she will!"

I suppose the most remarkable thing about the whole story is that Belk's Department Store is a good five miles from Katie's apartment.

The following Tuesday, the Bible class was alive with excitement. In walked a triumphant Margaret holding a smiling Katie's hand. As I began to share what I was learning about faith and the prayer of faith, I asked if anyone would like to openly declare her trust in Jesus Christ. Instantly Katie's arm shot up. She truly received Christ into her heart. Although a number of years have passed, whenever I ask Margaret about her sister, who no longer lives in the States, she lovingly says, "Katie is still trusting in my blessed Lord Jesus. I can't praise Him enough for bringing back her canary!"

Faith Is Learning to Pray

Through this experience I learned that when the salvation of a soul is at stake, God will do the impossible, if we will pray in faith. Yet, I would hasten to add, there is a wisdom to be learned about how to pray about certain trials. There must be a mature analysis of every difficulty before we can react in the proper attitude or pray in the right frame of mind. God will often answer the immature prayers of new believers, which He will not always do for those of us who have known Him longer. It is the same principle as when we give something to a baby, but withhold it from the older child because he has more wisdom and understanding of how we might feel about the matter.

To pray the prayer of faith, we must learn to hear the voice of our Lord when He speaks and understand His viewpoint concerning the matter. At times, we must learn to be quiet and wait on Him. The Psalmist said, "Be still and know that I am God" (Ps. 46:10). At times, we must learn to wait upon God and get a right diagnosis of the situation before we can pray according to His will.

When you go through a trial, first ask God to give you wisdom to understand why it is necessary because He says that only those who are exercised (proved by trial) by it receive the peaceable fruit of righteousness. Listen to the writer of the Book of Hebrews: "Now no chastening [no trial, no test] for the present seemeth to be joyous, but grievous; nevertheless, afterward it yieldeth the peaceable fruit of righteousness unto them which are exercised thereby" (Heb. 12:11).

We must learn to see what God is after in our lives. If someone has mistreated you, if you have been neglected in your home life or among your friends, or if you are going through a financial trial, learn how to pray about the situation. Ask God for wisdom.

At times, God will seem like an unkind friend. At other times it will seem like God is in complete darkness, and you will feel your prayers are only bouncing off the ceiling. Yet if you will learn to wait quietly upon the Lord and study His Word, He will in turn begin to reveal to you His own wisdom and will concerning your particular trial. We must remember the carnal (worldly) mind is anathema to God and is not subject to His will.

No amount of praying will be effective if the mind and heart are not truly surrendered to Jesus Christ. This is why Paul begged the Christians in Rome to give their all to God. He wanted them to know and understand the will of God for their lives. This is what he said to them: "I beseech you therefore, brethren, by the mercies of God, that ye present your bodies a living sacrifice, holy, acceptable unto God, which is your reasonable service. And be not conformed to this world; but be ye transformed by the renewing of your mind, that ye may prove what is that good, and acceptable, and perfect will of God" (Rom. 12:1, 2).

God wants you to develop your prayer life through your particular trial. He desires that you know and understand His will and His viewpoint. In order to transform a trial into a blessing, we must learn to get on our knees and ask God to give us His wisdom about what we are going through and why. You will discover, like many saints throughout the ages, that God is faithful. His Word never fails. He will establish your thoughts if you will ask in faith. Many times God will say, "I am putting you through this because there is something in your life I want taken out."

There is a difference between wisdom and knowledge. Wisdom, as someone has said, is to see life as a whole. It is an understanding of right and wrong, of good and evil. Many people have Bible knowledge but no wisdom. They know the Bible, can quote verses, yet have no wisdom or understanding of what the will of God is in a particular situation. This is why wisdom is so important to a believer, especially when he is going through a trial.

So, first of all, go to God and wait on Him for wisdom to understand His will. Only then can you pray according to His will—the only prayer He has promised to answer.

Many times we do not wait on God. We make our own decisions in the flesh according to what we desire, and then ask God to bless our decisions. We do not know how to seek for wisdom. This happens because we were not taught the importance of this particular admonition in the Scriptures. It is one thing to know the Bible, and quite another to understand God and what He is like.

To ask for wisdom implies humility of heart. If you think you have all the answers, you are never going to ask God for His wisdom. I can remember that when I first came to Christ and began to study His Word, I could explain everything about God. I could tell anyone exactly why God was allowing that particular thing in his or her life. I could quote Scripture after Scripture. You see, I had a great deal of knowledge but no wisdom. God says in Proverbs 9:10, "The fear of the Lord is the beginning of wisdom and the knowledge of the holy is understanding."

You could safely say that the fear of the Lord is not only reverential trust, but also accepting that God means what He says. There are no exceptions. It took me many years to learn that simple fact. When we do learn this, we are beginning to gain wisdom.

Much of our prayer life is wrong. God knows this. In fact, God says that we pray amiss in order to consume it upon our own lust (James 4:3). We are asking for things to satisfy ourselves. This is why we so desperately need to grow in wisdom and knowledge of God—so we can know His purpose and His will, and understand why we are going through the trials. Listen to Proverbs 2:1-6:

> My son, if thou wilt receive my words, and hide my commandments with thee; so that thou incline thine ear unto wisdom, and apply thine heart to understanding; Yea, if thou criest after knowledge, and liftest up thy voice for understanding; If thou seekest her as silver, and searchest for her as for hidden treasures; Then shalt thou understand the fear of the Lord, and find the knowledge of God. For the Lord giveth wisdom; out of his mouth cometh knowledge and understanding.

When we go through a trial, how many of us get on our knees and say, "O God, teach me in this what You want me to learn. Show me if there is anything in my life that needs to be straightened out so I can understand and know what You are after."

Most of us don't pray like that, however. We say, "Lord, help me! Get me out of this mess! Lord, I don't care what You do; just give me what I'm asking for!" That is not the way to transform a trial into a blessing.

There are many things in our lives we have asked God for, not caring how they came just so long as we got them. And then they turned into a curse instead of a blessing. We want to learn the wisdom of God through the prayer of faith. We want to learn a little bit more about our blessed God as we go through each trial. And as we go through the trials, we will learn. God will teach us if we want to be taught.

I was talking to an unhappy newlywed in Jacksonville, Florida. To every Scripture I gave her, she said, "Yes, I know that . . . I know that . . . I know that. . . . " I could not find one Scripture passage she did not know. Finally, I said, "Well, if you know all this Scripture, what are you doing about it? I mean, you are not acting on any of it, and yet you say you know it." This was another example of the difference between wisdom and knowledge. Wisdom is understanding God, not merely saying words or quoting Scripture. It is understanding the heart and will of God.

We must also keep in mind that God wants us to pray the prayer of *faith,* not simply pray. There is plenty of talking in God's direction, but it is not the prayer of faith. I know, because I have prayed so often like that—those desperate, panic prayers. There is no faith in that kind of praying whatsoever; just, "Lord, help! Help me!" And the Lord says, "I will never leave thee nor forsake thee, so that we may boldly say, the Lord is my helper" (Heb. 13:5, 6). "Yes, Lord; but I don't believe that right now! Just help me!"

I want to emphasize this because sometimes I believe you can talk yourself out of faith. I believe you can get hold of a situation and pray until you no longer believe God is going to answer you. You wrestle with it so long that faith flies out the window. Many times we ask God for a decision and then don't believe He will do it. That is why God says in James 1:6, "Let him ask in faith." Underline those words *in faith* in your Bible.

Many earnest believers desire wisdom from God, yet they have never understood that it comes only when they ask in faith. We must allow this truth to sink deep into our hearts. The unceasing principle of our entire Christian life is faith; it is the channel through which the Holy Spirit communicates the life and power and wisdom of God into the heart of man.

Faith is always taking God at His Word. God cannot lie. The blessedness of peace will enter your own life when, by faith, you realize that you do not have to strive or agonize to receive the wisdom of God, but simply believe that He will give it. All your own efforts to do so are useless; this is God's work, and we need only believe.

How often we look at our lack of faith rather than to His faithfulness. Faith is the vehicle that will remove the cloud from over your soul and allow the light of God's own wisdom and faithfulness to flood your longing heart with a peace that passes all understanding. Dare to believe! Dare to act upon that belief and you will discover the reality of God's own wisdom in your particular trial.

Prayer

Blessed Heavenly Father, how often we look at our lack of faith, instead of Your great faithfulness. We now ask for Your wisdom and thank You that You so wisely and carefully perfect that which concerns us. In Christ's name, Amen.

7

The Endurance of Faith

Happy is the man who doesn't give in and do wrong (endures) when he is tempted, for afterward he will get as his reward the crown of life that God has promised those who love him (James 1:12, TLB).

"Has God ever lost a star?" asked my son at the tender age of seven. How strange, I thought, that such a simple yet profound question should enter a child's mind. Together we searched the Scriptures; much to our delight, we discovered that God has never lost a single star. "He telleth the number of the stars, he calleth them all by their names" (Ps. 147:4).

It was thrilling for me to be reminded once again that God has never misplaced nor neglected one single thing throughout eternity; nor has he ever been too busy for the least things in His universe. For those of us who yearn to transform our trials into blessings, the assurance of this fact will ease our aching hearts. We begin to learn that God will keep us from falling as we go through trials if only we will trust Him completely.

The Elements of Enduring Faith

The last (and perhaps most important) way to change our problems into triumphs is through the endurance of faith. According to Webster's Dictionary, there is a difference between endurance and patience.

Endurance means, "the capability of lasting; continuance; the power of continuing under hardships without being overcome." The word *patience* means, "forbearance; enduring trials without complaining; calmness without being discontent; able to bear strain or stress."

We know God has promised that the trying of our faith will produce patience but endurance is a matter of the will. The inner attitude or reaction toward outward circumstances is the thing that matters most with God. The inner reaction determines the outward action. If God can purify us inside, what comes to the outside will be right. These inner attitudes and reactions are made up of all our emotions and thoughts and are directed by our will. Obviously we can't control all our circumstances, but we can control our reaction to them. It is in the will that the battle is fought and the victory won. If our will is to delight in the will of God and endure all trials as either coming from Him or allowed by Him, then we will have no argument with God concerning anything that comes. An unpleasant home situation, financial troubles, poor health, bad weather, bad politics—all of these will be accepted and endured as God's will for our life unless He sees fit to make a change, either in answer to believing prayer, or by His sovereign will.

There are different kinds of endurance. You can endure something by gritting your teeth and somehow getting through, but that is not the quality God is talking about. He means an endurance that counts it all joy—the only kind of endurance that glorifies God and is rewarded by Him. This is when we can say, "Thank you, Lord, for what You have allowed in my life just now. Praise You, dear Lord, that through this hard thing I am growing closer to You. Thank You for allowing me to go through this trial."

God has given us a guideline for enduring. The Scriptures reveal the source of our endurance and how we can go through a hard thing and still glorify God. Here is what God says:

> Looking unto Jesus, the author and finisher of our faith, who for the joy that was set before him endured the cross, despising the shame, and is set down at the right hand of the throne of God. For consider him that endured such contradiction of sinners against himself, lest ye be wearied and faint in your minds (Heb. 12:2, 3).

Our Lord Jesus Christ, for the joy that was set before Him, endured the cross. And what was that joy? Think of it! You and I, sinners, were the joy that was set before Him! We were the reason He endured the cross. He did not enjoy it. He despised the shame; yet He did it for you and me. The source of supply for our endurance is Jesus Christ Himself. If you merely endure something by gritting your teeth, you will lose your joy; but if you look into the face of Jesus Christ and say, "Lord, You endured even death for me—You went through agony for me—so I know I can endure this hard thing for Your sake. I know You are allowing it to develop my Christian character, so I thank You, Lord, and count it all joy." Thus, it is the attitude with which you endure that counts with God.

We might also call endurance a waiting faith. For example, read James 5:10, 11:

> Take, my brethren, the prophets, who have spoken in the name of the Lord, for an example of suffering affliction, and of patience. Behold, we count them happy which endure. Ye have heard of the patience of Job, and have seen the end of the Lord; that the Lord is very pitiful, and of tender mercy.

A waiting faith is one that can suffer a hardship, yet never give up, remaining patient, and ultimately glorifying God through it.

How much we need to learn to wait on Him. This is one of the things we lack the most in our Christian lives. We are living in a "now" generation, with "instant" everything. In the same way, we want to snap our fingers and have God answer us. How little we know about a waiting faith, about waiting on God for answers to prayer! James mentions the patience of Job. The quality of a patient, enduring, waiting faith is of great value to God. We need only look at Job's life to see this illustrated. How bountifully God restored him after his trial! How marvelously God poured out His blessings on this man!

True faith can wait and endure, can go through any hardship, any situation, and still believe God, still trust in Him and His faithfulness. True faith keeps on glorifying God and counts it all joy, no matter how bad the situation looks.

Along with endurance must come obedience, for this is the way we institute Christ as lord and master of our lives. Endurance through obedience is in itself a simple thing, yet among many believers there seems to be a lack of understanding of what this actually involves. Obedience and endurance are our main expressions of faith.

Every hero of faith mentioned in the Scriptures lived a life of endurance and obedience. Abraham was a man of faith because he obeyed God and endured to the end. His obedience to God and his trust in what God told him to do made Abraham a man of faith. It gave him the ability to endure. The true essence of faith is obedience to the Word of God, which helps us to endure and glorify God through any hardship.

In the Bible, obedience is equated with love: . . ."whoso keepeth his word, in him verily is the love of God perfected; hereby know we that we are in him" (I John 2:5).

Some have misinterpreted obedience to be the relationship of a slave to his master, and in a sense that is true. We know, however, that the apostle Paul and the other disciples declared themselves to be bondslaves by choice. They chose to obey their master. It was a relationship that resulted from their deep love for the Savior.

The writer to the Hebrews says of our Lord, "Though he were a Son, yet learned he obedience by the things which he suffered" (Heb. 5:8). Can anything less be required of His followers today? We can never learn love except through obedience, and we can never learn to endure unless we obey our Lord. Christ the eternal Son was equal with the Father, yet He obeyed His Father because of love.

It matters little how many times my sons tell me they love me if they do not obey me. By their obedience their love is manifested. Our Lord said, "If you love me you will keep my commandments" (John 14:15, RSV). True biblical obedience springs out of a heart of love. It is God's purpose that every one of His children should be conformed to the image of His Son, who obeyed from a heart of love. Yet you and I will never know this heart of love unless we obey. We can profess our faith and confess our love and proclaim our endurance, but without obedience it is empty.

But what if we don't have this heart of love for our Savior? What if our love is lukewarm, and we have no desire to obey, much less endure? Are we just as obligated to God when we feel inclined to do things another way? Are we compelled to be obedient to the Word of God? Is this the only way we will learn endurance?

An idea is spreading among some people that obedience to the Word of God is optional, that the necessity of obeying varies with the circumstances. This would mean that we are free to alter our course if the situation justifies it.

Others say obedience is a private matter concerning no one but the person involved. This attitude, of course, cannot be accepted by lovers of our Lord. We who belong to Him are His body, and each is, in a sense, responsible for the other. What each person does will affect other body members. We are not separate entities unto ourselves.

Until this passion of our Savior's love grips us and is infused into our hearts by the Holy Spirit, we will not be able to grasp this responsibility or learn how to endure in a way that pleases God. Obedience to God for the sake of others becomes a pure delight when we see our oneness with Jesus Christ and crown Him Lord of our lives.

It is here that we find the nobility of obedience and the true essence of endurance in our high calling of God in Christ Jesus. It was for others, you and me, that He was obedient to death. It was for our sake that He "endured such contradiction of sinners against himself" (Heb. 12:3). It is because of Him and His love for us that we can say, "For Your glory, Lord, I will obey You; not just for my own growth in grace, but for the sake of others also. For others, Lord, I will endure." Certainly the most noble expression of obedience to God is evident when it is poured out for the sake of others.

While obedience may be an act between myself and God, it will ultimately affect the lives of others. We have only to look at the life of Moses to learn this lesson. Every trivial act of obedience or disobedience committed by Moses affected the children of Israel. This is true in our own homes as well. Our obedience or disobedience to God affects the lives of our loved ones.

The Epistle to the Hebrews gives an account of the marvelous and extraordinary acts of courage, endurance, and faith of the heroes of Hebrew history. Obedient to their call, daring to obey God in the smallest details, deeply repentant when disobedient, they are examples of what God can do through those who are completely obedient to His Word.

It is also noteworthy that the word *obey* comes from a Latin compound, meaning that which you do in consequence to that which you hear. To live the Christ-filled life, to experience the reality of His presence, and to walk in the Spirit means that everything which touches the domain of our senses must always be placed under a sacred discipline of obedience, not only for our own spiritual growth but for the sake of others around us.

Lest you imagine that a life lived in obedience to the Word of God is tedious, let me say that unfailing obedience produces unfailing endurance, which, in turn, produces unfailing joy and peace. A joyless Christian is often a disobedient one. A life of obedience to the Word of God in the smallest details is one of fullest liberty, for where the Spirit of the Lord is—where He is recognized and obeyed even in the trivial details of life—there is joyous freedom.

As we think of these three ways to turn our trials into blessings—the acceptance, prayer, and endurance of faith—let us remember that God has a special crown for those who endure in the right way. I believe many of us are going to miss this crown because we murmur and complain about every hard thing that comes into our lives. Many times I have had tests and missed my crown of rejoicing because I complained.

Let me reflect for a moment about this crown of life mentioned in James 1:12. I do not believe God is talking here about the crown of eternal life. We know there is no way a person can lose eternal life once he has truly received Jesus Christ as his Savior, for He said, "No man can pluck you out of my hand" (John 10:28). No, you can't lose your salvation; but you can lose your crown. Many crowns are mentioned in the Bible. Some Christians will receive all of them, some very few. James 1:12 says you will receive a crown for the attitude and endurance you manifest when you go through a trial. Listen to Revelation 2:10: "Fear none of those things which thou shalt suffer; behold, the devil shall cast some of you into prison, that ye may be tried; and ye shall have tribulation ten days; be thou faithful unto death, and I will give thee the crown of life."

To endure a trial unto death would be the crowning victory for the child of God. Yet for us it may not be physical death as it was for those early saints. It will more likely be death to our selves—our desires, our ambitions, and our fear of what other people think. God says to us, "Be faithful to me unto death, and I will give you a crown of life"—abundant life, joyful, overflowing life!

In Revelation 3:11, Jesus says, "Behold I come quickly: hold that fast which thou hast, that no man take thy crown." He admonished us not to lose our crown. Learn to see in every trial an opportunity to win the crown that God has promised to them that love Him.

In the light of the world situation, the trials, sorrows, and injustices that will come upon us, what does God tell us? He says to be patient and remember that the King is coming!

God also says that only those who endure through earthly trials will be counted happy or joyful. This word *endurance,* as we have seen before, means a faith that can suffer and never give up. Reading the Book of Job, we discover that Job complained; he said he was miserable and wished he had never been born. Yet we see a faith in God that never gave up, a faith that cried out, "Though he slay me yet will I trust in him" (Job 13:15).

Through his troubles, Job grew in the reality of God, for he said, "I know that my Redeemer liveth. . . . in my flesh I shall see God" (Job 19:25a, 26b). And in the end, Job was blessed, proving that there is a real reward to those who endure.

Faith with this endurance quality is a faith like silver and gold that will endure through the fires and sorrows of life. Things happen in life that have no explanation—Job is a shining example. There was no real explanation for Job's suffering as he did. He did not know that he had been the subject of a contest between God and Satan. All he knew was that he was the recipient of terrible trials such as no man had ever known. Yet he was able to say in Job 23:10, "He knoweth the way that I take; when he has tried me, I shall come forth as gold."

Job had grown enough in his faith to know that God was the only solution to his problems. He was saying, "God knows the way I am taking. God knows I do not understand why this is happening, but I am going on. I am going to continue to trust Him; and in the end, I shall come forth as gold." There was faith involved in that statement. He was saying, "Lord, I know I am going to get through this trial, and I know that in the end I am going to glorify You in it."

Endurance must be a delight to God. In the end He was obviously pleased with Job because He commissioned Job to be a priest for the sake of his friends who had criticized him in his wretched condition. God set Job in a position to perform duties close to His heart.

Job not only was restored to his former estate, but he was able to glorify God through it. Job had endured with a waiting, obedient, crowning faith.

There is no way to please God without faith, regardless of how much we do for Him. The human mind often seems either unable or unwilling to grasp this simple fact. Yet all the attitudes of the Christian life must develop from this principle until it becomes a reality. The Bible says, "Without faith it is impossible to please him; for he that cometh to God must believe that he is, and that he is a rewarder of them that diligently seek him" (Heb. 11:6). Deeper knowledge of God comes from passing through the lonely valleys of trials and sufferings, for there we can discover the eternal secret that *God is*.

Looking into the Book of James, we discover that the theme of this small epistle is true faith. It was really written to Jewish believers who were undergoing much suffering, mostly at the hands of those within their own religion. Throughout church history, God's people have been persecuted, not only by unbelievers, but by those in their own churches as well. This kind of trial can be the hardest for a believer, yet our Lord Jesus Christ identifies with us through it all. He says, in essence, "Your faith is going to be tested, sometimes beyond what you think you can endure; but there is a crown waiting for you if you will accept this thing from Me. I want you to learn what real faith is all about."

Let us learn to wait on God, to wait and trust, no matter what comes. Even if God's answer is *no*, let us learn to accept His answer, be patient, and endure. Here alone lies the faith that overcomes the world of circumstances.

Sometimes God has to say *no*. This lesson came home to me in a forceful way when my boys were seven and eleven years old. My husband Don was to be out of town for a week on business. I assembled the boys and said, "This week Daddy will be gone, so you two can plan all the evening meals, and you can have anything you want."

"Really? You mean anything we want?" They were delighted.

Two days later I realized my mistake. Monday night we had hot dogs, french fried potatoes, and chocolate brownies with chocolate ice cream. Tuesday night it was pizza, coke, and a banana split. By Wednesday morning both boys were grumpy, and one complained that his stomach hurt. Wednesday night brought hamburgers, macaroni and cheese, and more french fries on the side. This brought more stomachaches, along with a headache, and "Do you think I ought to stay home from school in the morning?"

When Thursday night rolled around, I was not surprised when the suggestion was made, "Mother, how about you thinking up the dinner tonight? We don't feel so good."

That night we had a complete dinner of good vegetables and a tossed salad, with a large glass of milk. After dinner, baths, and good-night kisses, two contented little boys fell asleep.

As I was cleaning up the kitchen, God seemed to say to me, "My child, just as you cannot give your own children everything they ask for, there are times when I must say *no* to you."

And so we must learn to endure and accept even when God's answer is *no*. Learn to be patient. Establish your heart in God, even though all the circumstances around you may seem to be falling apart. Resolve deep in your will that you are going on with God, that you will glorify Jesus Christ no matter what trials or testings come into your life.

If you will begin to lay aside all anxiety about your circumstances and believe completely that your heavenly Father will wisely and carefully take care of everything that concerns you, the endurance of faith will come, and with it will come the rest of faith.

Instead of beginning the day burdened with the trials and problems in your life, joyfully transfer yourself and all your circumstances over to the care of your Father. Begin to love and praise and adore the Lord Jesus Christ. Give Him the preeminence in all your thoughts, desires, and motives. You will discover for yourself how to count it all joy when you go through trials.

I cannot describe the joy that will be yours when you wholeheartedly abandon the cares of your life to God and live moment by moment "looking unto Jesus, the author and finisher of our faith" (Heb. 12:2).

Prayer

O Lord, we would be altogether Yours. We would put You, and You only, first in our lives. May our only desire be that of pleasing You. May our lives be of such continuous joy that others will know that we have been in Your presence and will desire You for themselves. We praise You. We adore You. Thanks be unto God for His gift, our Lord Jesus Christ. Amen.